Sugar Gliders
or
Sugar Bears

Facts and Information

The complete guide to owning sugar gliders or
sugar bears including keeping as pets, care,
breeding, bonding, food, diet, lifespan, cages, toys,
accessories, costs and much more.

Acknowledgements

I would like to thank my wife and children for their endless love and support, especially my wife whose patience with me knows no bounds.

Foreword

The sugar glider is a small nocturnal marsupial that can be found living high up in the trees in Australia and the surrounding islands. Sugar gliders can also be found in homes all around the world as exotic pets. These little creatures are full of energy and make very entertaining pets, providing you care for them correctly. If you are considering a sugar glider as a pet, reading this book is the perfect place for you to start.

In this book you will learn the basics about sugar gliders including how to care for them, their nutritional requirements, health information and more. By the time you finish reading this book you will be ready to decide whether a sugar glider is the right pet for you and you will be well on your way in preparing to include one as part of your family.

Table of Contents

Chapter One: Introduction

When it comes to household pets, you are undoubtedly familiar with the standard options – cats, dogs, birds, hamsters, aquarium fish etc. How about non-standard and exotic pets like the sugar glider? Though it is technically a wild animal, the sugar glider has recently become extremely popular as a household pet, particularly in the United States. These furry little creatures are bred in captivity in large numbers for the pet trade and their popularity is increasing every day.

What makes sugar gliders so popular as pets? For some individuals it may be a novelty. Having a sugar glider as a pet is much more interesting than having a "standard" pet like a cat or dog. For many people, however, it is the playful and social nature of the cute sugar glider that makes them so endearing. These little creatures are full of energy and affection, making them highly entertaining as pets, though they do require a great deal more time and effort to care for than a normal pet.

If you are considering keeping sugar gliders as pets, this is the right book for you. In the entirety of this book, you will learn the basics about sugar gliders along with all the information you need to care for them.

1) Useful Terms to Know:

Arboreal – refers to an animal that spends most of its life in the trees.

Convergent Evolution – a term used when two unrelated species develop adaptations over time to fill a certain niche, becoming more similar to each other in the process.

Herbivore – An animal that follows a primarily plant-based diet.

Joey – the name given to a sugar glider baby; joeys is the term for multiple sugar glider babies.

Lineage – the lineal descent from an ancestor; the genealogic history of an individual.

Marsupial – a type of animal that carries its young in its pouch – examples of marsupial animals include kangaroos, wallabies, opossums and koala.

Nocturnal – refers to animals that are most active at night.

Omnivore – an animal that derives nutrition from both plant and meat-based food.

Patagium – a flexible membrane stretching between the front and back legs that assist an animal in gliding or flight

Topical Preventive – a medication applied to the skin (topically) to prevent fleas, ticks and other pests.

Chapter Two: Understanding Sugar Gliders

Because the sugar glider or sugar bear is technically an exotic pet, it is especially important that you carry out research before bringing one home. Caring for this type of pet is so different than keeping a dog or cat, so you want to be absolutely sure they are the right pet for you before you commit to one. In this chapter you will receive all the basic information you need to know about sugar gliders to allow you to make an informed decision. This chapter includes information about what exactly sugar gliders are and where they come from, as well as information about related species.

1) *What Are Sugar Gliders?*

If you have never seen one before picking up this book, you may be asking "what is a sugar glider?" or "what is a sugar bear?" The sugar glider, also known as the sugar bear, is a small, furry marsupial native to Australia. These creatures are actually a type of nocturnal gliding possum, named both for their ability to glide through the air and for their love of sugary fruits. Sugar gliders carry the scientific name *Petaurus breviceps* which translates from Latin to mean "short-headed rope-dancer." This name was given in reference to the aerial acrobatics these little creatures exhibit.

Sugar gliders look very similar to the flying squirrel and they display some similar habits but they are actually not closely related. The similarities between these two species are likely due to convergent evolution. These creatures are omnivorous and arboreal, found throughout the northern and eastern regions of Australia, they have also been introduced into Tasmania, Papua New Guinea, and other nearby islands.

The fact that these creatures are arboreal means they spend most of their lives in the trees. Sugar gliders build nests in tree hollows, feed from flowers that grow on the trees in their habitat, and glide between trees in search of food. It is also worth noting that sugar gliders are nocturnal by nature, which means that they are most active at night, spending much of the day sleeping in their nest.

Though sugar gliders are wild animals, in recent years they have started to become popular as pets. The size of these creatures is fairly small and they weigh approximately 4 to 5 ounces (113 to 142g), which makes them ideal for keeping in captivity. Sugar gliders are not endangered but they are one of the most commonly traded wild animals seen in the illegal pet trade. When bred in captivity, however, sugar gliders are completely legal as pets as long as the owner obtains the appropriate permit or license.

In addition to being beautiful wild animals, sugar gliders make very interesting pets, which is why they are so popular. Not only do these creatures have a very unique appearance, but they can also be very entertaining. If you are looking for an exotic pet, the sugar glider is well suited to being kept in captivity. However sugar gliders are exotic pets and are not right for everyone. You should therefore take the time to learn everything you can about them before you decide to bring one home.

In this book you will discover the basics about sugar gliders, both in the wild and in captivity, enabling you to make an educated decision regarding whether or not this is the right pet for you. You will receive basic information about the species as well as the answers to some of your most pressing questions including:

- Are sugar gliders good pets?
- How many sugar gliders should I own?
- What do sugar gliders eat?
- What kind of cage do sugar gliders require?
- What sugar glider toys do I need?
- How do I keep my sugar gliders healthy?

2) Facts About Sugar Gliders

It has already been mentioned that sugar gliders are small, nocturnal marsupials native to northern and eastern Australia. A marsupial is a species of animal that carries its young in its pouch, examples include kangaroos, wallabies, opossums and koala. Sugar gliders have soft, thick fur that is blue-grey in color, fading to cream on the throat and chest and typically a black stripe running from the nose to about halfway down the back. There are also some sugar gliders that exhibit yellow or tan coloring as well as albino variations, though these are extremely rare.

Sugar gliders are small and have bodies like squirrels with a long prehensile tail. The male of the species is usually larger than the female, though neither will grow much larger than 12 inches (30.5cm) in length, including the tail. The tail of a sugar glider may measure as much as 7 to 8 inches (17.8 to 20.3cm) of its total body length. Male sugar gliders weigh 4 to 5.6 oz. (115 to 160g) whilst females weigh 3.3 to 4.75 oz. (95 to 135g).

Given the fact that sugar gliders are nocturnal, they have very large eyes that enable them to see at night. Their ears are able to swivel which assists the animal to locate its prey even when there is a lack of visibility. Sugar gliders have five toes on each foot, each bearing a small sharp claw except for the opposable toe on each of the two hind feet. The second and third toes on the hind feet are partially syndactylous, or fused, to form a type of grooming comb that the sugar glider will use to keep it's coat clean.

Perhaps the most interesting physical feature of the sugar glider is its patagium – the membrane that extends from the fifth toe on the front foot to the first toe on the hind foot. When the sugar glider stretches its legs, the patagium forms a kind of parachute that enables the animal to glide through the air across considerable distances. Much like the flying squirrel, the sugar glider cannot achieve actual flight. Firstly, it runs to pick up speed then jumps from a branch and glides, using the patagium to prolong its glide.

How do Sugar Gliders Glide?

You have already learned that sugar gliders possess a special membrane called a patagium. This enables them to glide through the air but you will never see a sugar glider flying. So how exactly does the patagium work? The patagium is a stretchy and flexible flap of skin that increases the animal's surface area, catching the air and acting as a sort of parachute and slows the sugar glider's descent. In the wild, sugar gliders have been known to glide over 164 feet (50 meters) at one time. To prepare for their glide, sugar gliders jump, spreading and extending their legs to open the patagium. By moving their arms and legs, sugar gliders control airflow which gives them control over their speed and direction.

a) Summary of Sugar Glider Facts

- Scientific name is *Petaurus breviceps.*
- Belongs to marsupial infraclass.
- Related to various gliding possum species.
- Arboreal and nocturnal by nature.
- Has large eyes, swivel ears, prehensile tail, syndactylous toes, patagium.
- Fur is soft and thick.
- Color is blue-grey, fading to cream on the chest and throat.
- Typical markings include a black stripe from nose halfway down the back.
- Color variations may include yellow, tan or albino (very rare).
- Average body length is 5 to 6 inches (12.7 to 15.2cm).
- Average tail length is 7 to 8 inches (17.8 to 20.3cm).
- Average weight for males is 4 to 5.6 oz. (115 to 160g).
- Average weight for females is 3.3 to 4.75 oz. (95 to 135g).
- Average sugar glider lifespan is up to 9 years in the wild, up to 12 years in captivity.
- Diet in the wild consists of insects, small vertebrates, fruit and tree sap.

3) History of Sugar Gliders

The origins of the sugar glider can be traced all the way back to the first marsupials which originate from a group of mammals called metatherians. It is generally thought that the last common ancestor of modern marsupials split from placental mammals during the mid-Jurassic period. Evidence of this theory arises from fossil metatherians that can be distinguished from placental mammals (called eutherians) by their teeth. Metatherians possess four pairs of molars while eutherians have no more than three pairs. Judging by fossil evidence, the earliest metatherian was *Sinodelphys szalayi* in China over 125 million years ago.

The earliest known marsupial fossil belongs to *Peradectes minor*, originating in Laurasia approximately 65 million years ago. With the splitting of Pangea, marsupials spread to South America where various forms of possum evolved. The ancestors of Australian marsupials like the sugar glider are thought to have arrived in Australia via Antarctica sometime around 50 million years ago just after the two landmasses split. Recent DNA analysis performed in 2010 confirms that all living marsupials share common South American ancestors.

a) Sugar Glider vs. Flying Squirrel

It has already been mentioned that the sugar glider is not closely related to the flying squirrel, but you may be curious about how two animals with so many obvious similarities could be unrelated. It is a simple case of convergent evolution. Convergent evolution is a term used when two unrelated species develop adaptations over time to fill a certain niche, becoming more similar to each other in the process. This is most likely to occur when similar niches are found in two different geographical locations for example, Australia and North America.

The sugar glider (*Petaurus breviceps*) is native to Australia while two species of North American flying squirrel belong to the genus *Glaucomys*. Both animals possess a patagium that enables them to glide through the air from one tree to another. The flying squirrel and the sugar glider are very similar in size and appearance and both are arboreal and nocturnal. If you trace their taxonomy, however, you will find that they belong to completely different taxonomical orders. In fact, the sugar glider belongs to an infraclass (marsupial) within the Mammalia class.

4) Sugar Gliders in the Wild

When you see a sugar glider in captivity, you may ask yourself "what is the sugar glider's natural habitat?" The sugar glider is native to Australia, found in forested areas throughout the northern and eastern regions of the continent. In 1835, the species was introduced to Tasmania and small colonies can also be found on Papua New Guinea and other islands in the area such as the Louisiade Archipelago and the Bismarck Archipelago. Though sugar gliders tend to inhabit any forested area that has an adequate food supply, they are most commonly found in forests where eucalyptus trees are plentiful.

Wild sugar gliders prey on insects and small vertebrates as well as the sweet sap of gum, acacia and eucalyptus trees. Natural predators of sugar gliders include kookaburras, goannas, snakes, quolls, native owls and feral cats. When enough food is available, sugar gliders can be found in a density of approximately 1 per 1,000 square meters (0.62 square miles).

In their natural habitat, sugar gliders typically go through a period of torpor during the cold season. Torpor is similar to hibernation in that the animal becomes immobile and unresponsive, but it generally only lasts for a day or two at a time. Sugar gliders are most likely to go into torpor when it gets cold, during periods of drought, on very rainy nights, or simply when it is inactive. During torpor, the sugar glider's body temperature drops in order to reduce energy expenditure, this is particularly important during periods of drought when food is scarce. As a small animal, sugar gliders have very active metabolisms and are very energetic, so torpor helps to reduce their energy expenditure when there isn't enough food to replenish fuel stores.

5) Related Species

Given the fact that all Australian marsupials evolved from South American marsupials, you can assume that many of them would be related. In fact, the sugar glider is similar to a number of other Australian species in either appearance or habits. Below you will find a list of species related to the sugar glider as well as an overview of how the two species compare:

- Squirrel Glider (*Petaurus norfolcensis*)
- Mahogany Glider (*Petaurus gracilis*)
- Greater Glider (*Petauroides volans*)
- Feathertail Glider (*Acrobates pygmaeus*)
- Yellow-Bellied Glider (*Petaurus australis*)

Squirrel Glider (*Petaurus norfolcensis*)

The squirrel glider belongs to the same genus as the sugar glider and it, too, is native to Australia. In comparison to the sugar glider, the squirrel glider is about twice the size and weighs up to ½ lb. (230g). These creatures have a similar color to the sugar glider and follow a comparable diet.

Mahogany Glider (*Petaurus gracilis*)

Mahogany gliders are larger than sugar gliders, growing up to 10.4 inches (26.5cm) in the body alone and weighing up to 0.9 lbs. (410g). This species also has a much smaller natural range and is considered a threatened species.

Greater Glider (*Petauroides volans*)

Though not as closely related to the sugar glider, the greater glider exhibits very similar habits and physical characteristics. Greater gliders grow up to 17 inches (43 cm) long with a tail length of up to 21 inches (53 cm). Unlike sugar gliders, the greater glider is completely herbivorous.

Feathertail Glider (*Acrobates pygmaeus*)

The feathertail glider is much smaller than a sugar glider and is the size of a small mouse, growing up to 3.14 inches (80mm) and weighing up to 0.5 oz. (14g). Though the feathertail glider possesses the same kind of patagium as the sugar glider, the feathertail glider's patagium is much thicker and smaller in proportion.

Yellow-Bellied Glider (*Petaurus australis*)

Yellow-bellied gliders are similar in size to a rabbit, growing up to 11.8 inches (30cm) long with an additional 19 inches (48cm) of tail. As suggested by the name, yellow-bellied gliders have yellowish coloration on their bellies and contrasts with the dark grey-brown fur on its back.

Chapter Three: What to Know Before You Buy

Because sugar gliders are exotic pets, there are a great many factors you need to consider before bringing one home. For example, you need to determine whether it is legal for you to keep a sugar glider as a pet in your area and how sugar gliders will fare with your other pets, whether they are better kept singly or in pairs, and the average price of sugar gliders. All of this practical information about sugar glider care will be provided within this chapter.

1) Do You Need a License?

Sugar gliders are not considered a threatened or endangered species, so you do not have to worry about the morality of keeping them as pets as long as you purchase sugar gliders that have been legally captive-bred. It is illegal to keep sugar gliders that have been taken from the wild as pets unless you are part of a rescue agency or have a special license to do so. However, captive-bred sugar gliders require a special permit or license to keep. In this section you will learn the basics about licensing requirements for sugar gliders as pets in both the U.S. and the U.K.

Note: The information regarding licensing requirements for sugar gliders may change over time.

a) Licensing in the U.S.

In the United States there are very strict laws regarding the sale and keeping of exotic pets such as the sugar glider. For most part, however, these laws are issued at the state rather than federal level. This means that it may be perfectly legal to own a sugar glider as a pet in one state while it is forbidden in another. Until recently, there were only four

U.S. states that did not permit sugar gliders as pets –
California, Georgia, Massachusetts and Pennsylvania. The
state of Georgia recently issued legislation to legalize the
keeping of sugar gliders as pets, therefore only three states
remain in which sugar gliders are not permitted.

Even if you live in a state where sugar gliders are
permitted, you still have to obtain a permit or license to
keep them. Contact your local council to determine the
licensing requirements for sugar gliders in your state and
to obtain the paperwork for licensing. Keep in mind that
you will need a different license if you intend to breed or
sell your sugar gliders. Sugar glider breeders in the U.S. are
required to have a USDA license if they possess more than
three intact females under new law (this also includes other
animals besides sugar gliders).

For example, if you have three intact female sugar gliders
you may not be required to obtain a USDA license. If,
however, you have 3 intact female sugar gliders and an
intact female of any other animal (even if it is not used for
breeding), you will need to obtain a license.

Note: Laws do change so please check with your local council for the
latest rules and regulations.

How to: Obtaining a USDA Sugar Glider License

The steps below are provided to help give you an insight into the process of obtaining a sugar glider permit might be like in the U.S. Specific licensing requirements and the process to obtain them will differ from one state to another, so the steps below serve only as an example. These are the steps required to obtain a USDA license if you plan to keep more than 3 female sugar gliders:

1. Contact your local regional USDA office or visit their website to request an information packet about the license.
2. Review the enclosed materials when it arrives (allow 1 to 2 weeks) and contact the office with any questions you may have.
3. Decide which license you want to apply for:
   - Class A – Allows you to sell animals you have raised yourself.
   - Class B – Allows you to broker, or sell, animals raised by someone else.
   - Class C – Strictly for exhibition only.
4. Fill out the request form for the license you have chosen and mail it to your local regional office along with the appropriate filing fee.

5. Schedule an appointment with your vet and ask him to complete the Program of Veterinary Care form.

6. Follow up with the USDA to schedule your inspection – review the requirements the inspector will be using to evaluate your establishment.

7. Complete your inspection and receive your customer ID number from the inspector.

8. Expect to receive your certificate and license in the mail 2 to 3 weeks later.

b) Licensing in the U.K.

Licensing requirements for pets in the U.K. are very different than in the United States. Though the keeping of exotic and endangered animals as pets is strictly regulated, captive-bred animals like sugar gliders generally do not require any sort of permit or license. The main piece of legislation you need to be aware of in the U.K. is the Animal Welfare Act of 2006. This act requires pet owners to provide for the basic needs of pets including the following:

- A suitable environment.
- A suitable diet.
- The ability to exhibit normal behavior.
- Being housed with (or apart from) other animals.
- Protection from pain, suffering, injury and disease.

You should also be aware of the strict regulations regarding the transportation of animals into and out of the U.K. If you are moving to or from the U.K. and plan to bring your sugar gliders with you, you may need to obtain and Animal Moving License (AML) and your sugar gliders may need to be kept in quarantine for a period of time before you can take them into your home. These measures were put in place to prevent the spread of disease in the U.K., primarily rabies, which was eradicated in the U.K. in the early 20th century.

2) Pet Insurance for Sugar Gliders

When you are considering bringing a new pet into the home, one of the most important things you should take into account is whether you are able to cover its costs for food and veterinary care. Animals such as cats and dogs require annual or semi-annual check-ups as well as various vaccinations and preventives. Sugar gliders, on the other hand, do not require any vaccinations and rarely require veterinary care as long as you provide them with a safe environment and a healthy diet.

In the event of an illness or injury, however, providing veterinary care for your sugar glider will be much more expensive than it would be for a cat or dog. This is because you will have to take your sugar glider to an exotic vet – not all veterinarians are qualified or licensed to care for exotic pets such as sugar gliders. The cost for a basic examination from an exotic vet will be higher than that of a traditional vet and any services your sugar glider requires, such as x-rays, blood work and surgery, will also be more expensive.

If you are concerned about being able to cover the cost of emergency veterinary services for your sugar glider, you may want to think about pet insurance. Pet insurance works in a very similar way to health insurance for humans. In exchange for a monthly fee (premium), you receive insurance cover for certain services. Whereas health insurance for humans usually enables you to pay a co-pay for services rather than paying the entire cost upfront, pet insurance generally offers reimbursement for covered services. The cost for having pet insurance for your sugar gliders will vary depending which company you choose, but it may be something you should consider if you are worried about being able to afford the cost of emergency treatment.

Some examples of pet insurance companies that cover sugar gliders include:

U.S. Websites:

Pet Assure

www.petassure.com

Veterinary Pet Insurance

www.petinsurance.com

U.K. Websites:

Petplan – Exotic Direct

www.exoticdirect.co.uk

Cliverton Exotic Pet and DWAA Insurance

www.cliverton.co.uk

3) How Many Should You Buy?

In their natural habitat, sugar gliders often live in family groups that consist of up to seven adults as well as past season's young. All adults in the colony participate in defending the nest and also engage in social grooming. There is typically a dominant male in the group that will mark both his territory and the members of the group with his scent – this helps to identify intruders.

When keeping sugar gliders as pets, it is important to recognize the social requirements of this species. Even though they are living in captivity, pet sugar gliders still need to be kept in groups or pairs in order for them to be truly happy. In addition to having other sugar gliders to interact with, these creatures also require frequent personal interaction with their owners that will help to keep your sugar gliders tame and will solidify the bond with your pets ensuring they remain affectionate towards you.

4) Can Sugar Gliders Be Kept with Other Pets?

If you already own other pets, you may be concerned about bringing sugar gliders into your home. Sugar gliders are, after all, small rodent-like creatures that cats and dogs may see as prey. You may be surprised to learn, however, that sugar gliders are highly compatible with other household pets. In fact, if you raise the sugar gliders from babies, they are likely to form lifelong bonds with other pets in your household.

How is this possible? Whilst sugar gliders may look like rodents, they are actually marsupials, which means that they do not smell like food to for example, your cat or dog. Sugar gliders also do not act like prey, so your other pets may simply not know what to make of them. Due to their social and playful nature, your sugar gliders will engage with the other pets in your house and before long will form a bond of friendship. This isn't to say that you can simply bring a sugar glider into the house and not expect your cat or dog to chase it. If you introduce your new pets gradually and in a protected and correct manner, other pets in your home should get along with your sugar gliders just fine.

5) *Ease and Cost of Care*

Before you purchase a sugar glider, you need to be sure that you can manage the financial responsibility of keeping them as pets. Because sugar gliders are so small, the cost for food is not significant but you have to consider the initial purchasing costs and charges for veterinary care etc. In this section you will learn what to expect in terms of initial and monthly costs of keeping sugar gliders as pets.

a) Initial Costs

The initial costs for keeping sugar gliders include the expense you must cover to bring your sugar gliders home. You may for instance be wondering, "how much are sugar gliders?" The purchase of the sugar gliders is one initial cost to consider in addition to the cost of the cage, toys and accessories. Below you will find an estimation and explanation of initial costs.

Purchase Price – The sugar glider price will vary depending where you buy them and what color variation you choose. Purchasing a standard sugar glider from a licensed breeder is estimated to cost between $100 and $300

(£65 to £195). However, if you choose to buy one of the non-standard color variations, the cost could be upwards of $500 (£325) each.

Cage – Again, the cost for your sugar glider's cage will vary depending which option you go with. In order to provide your sugar gliders with adequate space for climbing and playing, the cage will need to be fairly large. You will also need to take into account that many standard commercial pet cages will not meet the requirements for sugar gliders so you may need to consider a custom built cage. For the sake of budgeting costs, you should expect to pay between $150 and $300 (£98 to £195).

Toys/Accessories – Sugar gliders are very active animals so they will require a variety of toys and accessories in their cage, for example, wheels, nesting pouches, ropes and branches. More examples are provided in Chapter Five. For the sake of budgeting your costs, plan to spend about $100 to $200 (£65 to £130) on high-quality toys and accessories for your sugar glider cage.

Note: Because it is recommended that you keep sugar gliders in pairs or groups, the table on the following page includes the costs for one sugar glider, for two sugar gliders and for a trio.

Initial Costs for Sugar Gliders

Costs	One	Two	Three
Purchase	$100 to $300 (£65 to £195)	$200 to $600 (£130 to £390)	$300 to $900 (£195 to £585)
Cage	$150 to $300 (£98 to £195)	$150 to $300 (£98 to £195)	$150 to $300 (£98 to £195)
Accessories	$100 to $200 (£65 to £130)	$100 to $200 (£65 to £130)	$100 to $200 (£65 to £130)
Total*	**$350 to $800 (£228 to £520)**	**$450 to $1,100 (£293 to £715)**	**$550 to $1,400 (£358 to £910)**

*The prices and exchange rates used in this book were current at the time of publication but may change over time.

b) Monthly Costs

The monthly costs for sugar gliders are fairly low in comparison to other pets. You do, however, need to be prepared to cover the cost of food, bedding, replacement toys and veterinary care on a regular basis. Below you will find an explanation of the monthly outlay for sugar gliders as well as an estimate for each.

Food – For the most part, sugar gliders will eat food that you already buy for yourself for example, fresh fruit, vegetables, etc. It may also be prudent to buy pellet food specially formulated for sugar gliders to have at hand to provide a vital protein source. Animal protein (such as chicken and beef) can give sugar gliders a musty smell. Because you won't actually be buying much food specifically for your sugar glider, you shouldn't have to pay more than $10 (£6.50) a month on food.

Bedding – This is an optional cost because if you have a sugar glider cage with bars on the bottom you may not need bedding to help absorb waste. If you choose to use bedding in your sugar glider cage, however, a large bag of pine shavings will cost you less than $15 (£9.75) and will last about a month.

Replacement Toys – Because sugar gliders have sharp teeth and claws, you should expect their toys to wear out over time. You may not need to replace their toys every month, but you should budget for unexpected expenses such as repairs or replacements for cage accessories. For the sake of budgeting, plan for approximately $10 (£6.50) per month.

Veterinary Care – Again, veterinary care is not something that you should expect to pay for each and every month. In fact, you may never have to take your sugar glider to the vet unless he gets injured or falls ill. The cost for an examination by an exotic vet is usually about $60 (£39) so, if you take your sugar glider to the vet once per year, the approximate monthly cost is $5 (£3.25).

Monthly Costs for Sugar Gliders

Costs	One	Two	Three
Food	$10 (£6.50)	$20 (£13)	$30 (£19.50)
Bedding	$15 (£9.75)	$15 (£9.75)	$15 (£9.75)
Replacements	$10 (£6.50)	$10 (£6.50)	$10 (£6.50)
Vet Care	$5 (£3.25)	$10 (£6.50)	$15 (£9.75)
Total*	**$40 (£26)**	**$55 (£35.75)**	**$70 (£45.50)**

*The prices and exchange rates used in this book were current at the time of publication but may change over time.

6) Pros and Cons of Sugar Gliders

As is true for all household pets, there are pros and cons to keeping sugar gliders. Before you decide whether or not this is the right pet for you, you would do well to consider both the positive and negative aspects of sugar gliders as pets. Below you will find a basic list of pros and cons for the species as well as a comparison of keeping male versus female sugar gliders.

Pros for Sugar Gliders as Pets

- Small size means they don't take up a lot of space.
- They do not require supplements if fed a healthy and balanced diet.
- Do not eat large quantities of food.
- When properly tamed, they can become quite affectionate with owners.
- Generally get along well with other household pets (except snakes and birds).
- Can be carried around in your pocket (normally unlikely to have "accidents").
- Generally not odorous if the cage is cleaned regularly and the correct diet is provided.

Cons for Sugar Gliders as Pets

- Must be kept in pairs or groups due to their highly social nature.
- Will require plenty of handling from a young age to remain tame around people.
- Require many hours of attention and interaction on a daily basis .
- Most active at night – this is when they will crave attention and affection.
- Require an exotic vet for care – may be more expensive than a traditional vet.
- Prone to calcium deficiencies in captivity if not fed a balanced diet.
- Can be fairly expensive to buy compared to other pets – may cost between $100 and $300 (£65 to £195).
- You will need to glider-proof your home for their safety (keep windows shut, toilet lids down, etc.).
- They are a long-term commitment, living beyond 12 years when properly cared for.

a) Male vs. Female Sugar Gliders

Pros/Cons for Female Sugar Gliders

- If you keep more than 3 intact females, you may need to obtain a USDA license in the U.S.
- Less likely to have a musky odor than males
- Less territorial than males.
- More shy than males, especially around strangers, but more affectionate with owners.
- Generally not recommended for altering (spaying) due to their complex reproductive system.
- Should not be kept with intact males unless you are breeding them.

Pros/Cons for Male Sugar Gliders

- Possess scent glands on the head, chest and anus and therefore they may have a slightly musky odor.
- Should not be paired with other intact males or with intact females unless you are breeding them.
- Neutered males have less odor and tend to be more docile.
- May be dominant around other males and likely to mark territory.

- Often more outgoing and curious around new people, more likely to form bonds.

Chapter Four: Purchasing Sugar Gliders

By now you should have a pretty good idea whether a sugar glider is the right pet for you. Before you make your final decision however, you should consider where you are going to buy your sugar gliders. Purchasing a sugar glider is not as simple as choosing one at the local pet store, you may have to locate and buy from a licensed breeder. In this chapter you will learn the basics about purchasing sugar gliders as well as tips for selecting a baby sugar glider that looks healthy.

1) *Where to Buy Sugar Gliders*

Buying a sugar glider is a little more complicated than just stopping in to your local pet store. Few pet stores are likely to have sugar bears for sale and, even if they do, you cannot be entirely sure that the store is licensed to sell them. If you plan on purchasing sugar gliders your best option is to buy directly from a licensed breeder. In this section you will find tips for locating a licensed sugar glider breeder that has sugar gliders for sale in both the U.S. and the U.K.

a) Buying in the U.S.

Because the breeding and selling of sugar gliders is so strictly regulated in the U.S. you will need to be very careful from where you acquire your sugar gliders. If you do not obtain them from a licensed breeder (and if you do not have the proper license yourself), you may run the risk of your beloved pets being confiscated. Referring back to the information in the previous chapter, any sugar glider breeder you buy from should hold a USDA license if they possess more than three intact breeding females. Even if the breeder is not legally required to obtain a license under the new law, a reputable breeder will most likely be licensed anyway.

There are several ways you can begin the search for a sugar bear for sale in the United States. You are unlikely to see them in your local pet store, but it is fairly easy to find local breeders. In performing an online search for sugar glider breeders, you are likely to return a variety of results. Another option and perhaps a better one, is to consult a list of licensed sugar glider breeders and to find one nearest to you. You can find this list through the Animal and Plant Health Inspection Service (APHIS) which is part of the United States Department of Agriculture (USDA).

Alternatively you can find a database of sugar glider breeders by state from the below website. Ensure you check for USDA licenses.

www.sugargliderhelp.com

b) Buying in the U.K.

As in the United States, it is recommended in the U.K. that you purchase your sugar gliders from an experienced breeder. You may be able to find a sugar glider for sale from hobby breeders that are less expensive, but you need to consider whether this is worthwhile. With a hobby breeder you cannot be sure of the quality of the breeding stock or the health status of the parents. Both these issues may adversely affect the sugar glider and therefore it is best to go with a reputable breeder.

Here are some links for sugar glider breeders in the U.K.:

Sugar Glider Breeder Directory
www.sugarglider-breeder.co.uk

Southwest Sugar Gliders
www.southwest-sugargliders.co.uk

East Coast Gliders
www.eastcoastgliders.co.uk

North East Gliders and Exotics
www.northeast-sugargliders.co.uk

Note: Avoid purchasing sugar gliders online and only purchase from experienced and licensed breeders. Purchasing animals online involves subjecting them to the shipping process during which they may be exposed to severe conditions and rough handling. This is unethical, unfair and could be considered animal cruelty and therefore should be avoided. Additionally, you want to see the sugar glider you are purchasing before you agree to buy it.

2) *How to Select a Healthy Sugar Glider*

As you would with any pet, it is recommended that you actually visit the breeder and select your sugar glider in person. This is the best way to ensure that you end up with a sugar glider well suited to your personality – it also gives you a chance to ensure the sugar glider is healthy without having to just take the breeder's word for it. When you visit the breeder, follow these steps to picking out a healthy sugar glider Joey:

- Ask to tour the facilities when you arrive – many sugar glider breeders operate from their home and if so, they still should have an organized system for keeping the breeding stock and raising the joeys.

- Take a look at the parents of the Joey you are considering to make certain it is in good health.

- Ask the breeder plenty of questions to determine their experience in breeding sugar gliders.

- Ask about a health guarantee and any kind of "after-sale" support the breeder may offer.

- Check to ensure the breeder is licensed – in the U.S., breeders that have more than 3 intact females must carry a USDA license.

- Make sure the joeys offered by the breeder are at least 8 weeks old - never buy a Joey less than 8 weeks out of the pouch.

- Thoroughly inspect the joeys – they should have bright eyes and bushy tails, showing curiosity at your arrival.

- Make sure the joeys are fully weaned – they should not be suckling from the mother at all any more.

- Check the Joey's stools for firm formation (if they are not, it could be an indication of poor health).

- Be wary of sugar gliders that appear to be frightened of humans or attempt to run away.

- Keep in mind that personality will vary from one sugar glider to another, so choose one with a temperament that fits your personality.

Chapter Five: Caring for Sugar Gliders

Now that you are familiar with the practical aspects of preparing for and purchasing sugar gliders, you are ready to learn the details of their care. In this chapter you will receive valuable sugar glider information about preparing your sugar glider cage and formulating a healthy diet for your new pets. You will also obtain tips for understanding sugar glider behavior, taming and handling. The more knowledge you absorb from this chapter on owning a sugar glider before bringing one home, the better equipped you will be.

1) Habitat Requirements

Sugar gliders are very social animals and will want to spend a great deal of time out of their cage interacting with you. During the day, your sugar glider will be content to sleep in the pocket of your jacket or rest on your shoulder. However when you are not interacting with your sugar glider, you will need to keep him in a large cage that provides him with plenty of space and toys to play with. In this section you will learn the basics about setting up and maintaining a cage for your glider.

a) Preparing the House and Cage

Because sugar gliders are very curious, it is important that you prepare your home for your sugar glider's safety. Make sure all doors and windows are kept closed when your sugar glider is out of his cage and do not leave any open containers of water. Whilst your sugar glider can swim if necessary, he may have trouble getting out of polished containers (such as metal pet water bowls) and may become exhausted and drown. You should also take care to store chemicals, cleaning products and toxic foods away from your sugar glider's reach.

When selecting a cage for your sugar glider, there are a number of important factors to consider: size, shape and material. Though sugar gliders are very small, they are also highly active and will need plenty of room to play. The minimum recommended size for a sugar glider cage is 24 x 24 x 36 inches (61 x 61 x 91.4cm). The cage should be at least 24 inches (61cm) deep and wide with a height of at least 36 inches (91.4cm). The height of the cage is particularly important so your gliders can jump around. This size applies to a pair of sugar gliders. If you plan to keep three or more, a larger cage will be necessary.

The ideal cage for sugar gliders is made of metal wire or wire mesh, which will enable your gliders to climb. If you choose a cage with metal bars, make sure the spacing is no more than ½ inch (1.27cm) so that your sugar glider cannot squeeze through. It is also important the bars are horizontal rather than vertical so they provide your sugar glider with toeholds for climbing.

In addition to considering the size, shape and materials for your sugar glider cage, there are also some practical aspects to consider. Many sugar glider owners prefer cages that have a base of metal bars or mesh to allow waste and dropped food to fall through into a collection tray.

Alternatively, you can use a solid-based cage and line it with soft bedding such as pine shavings to absorb urine. If you do use sugar glider bedding, make sure to replace it at least once a week and more often if you have several sugar gliders.

How to: Glider-Proofing Your Home:

If you plan to allow your sugar glider out of his cage, you need to be sure that your home is safe. You should always keep an eye on your sugar glider when he is out of the cage, but following these tips will help to ensure he is unlikely to get into danger or difficulty while he is "out and about" in your home:

- Select one room of your house and only let your sugar glider loose in that room (with the door closed).
- Cover all electrical sockets with plastic safety covers.
- Keep all household chemicals stored away.
- Ensure the lid to your toilet is kept closed at all times so your sugar glider doesn't get stuck and drown.
- Avoid leaving bowls or glasses of water around.
- Always keep doors and windows tightly closed.
- Remove any houseplants that could be toxic.

- Attend to any tiny crevices where your glider might hide by blocking them up.

b) Toys and Accessories

Whilst the bars of your sugar glider's cage will provide them with endless amusement in the form of climbing, there are some sugar glider toys you may want to introduce. One of the most important sugar glider accessories to include in your sugar glider cage is a nest box where your sugar glider can sleep during the day. Ideally, a nest box should be made of porous materials such as wood or unglazed clay that will absorb moisture and breathe. The disadvantage of this option of nest box is it will absorb urine, so will need to be replaced on a regular basis.

Perhaps a more practical choice of nest box is plastic, which is easy to clean and inexpensive. To prevent your sugar gliders from defecating on the top of the box, install it against the ceiling of the cage. Another option for nest boxes is a cloth pouch, not only are these items very comfortable for your sugar glider, but can also be washed as often as needed. If you decide not to use a cloth nesting box, make sure some soft bedding is provided in the nest box for your sugar gliders.

Other toys and accessories to include in your sugar glider cage are:

- Branches for climbing.
- Rope or wooden ladders.
- Wooden bird toys.
- A sugar glider wheel (for exercise).
- Food and water dishes.
- Water bottle.
- Heating rock (optional).

Making your own toys and accessories for your sugar glider cage may be easier than you think and is a great way to save money. The best material suitable for homemade sugar glider cage accessories is felt which can be cut into a variety of shapes and the pieces put together without any sewing required. Make a hammock for your sugar glider by cutting a triangular shaped piece of felt to fit in the corner of the cage then attach it to the walls with strips of felt. Braided lengths of felt can be used as a carrying strap for a homemade bonding pouch or as ropes and ladders in the cage. Felt can be found in a variety of colors and patterns, at your local craft store.

How to: Simulating a Natural Environment

Because your sugar bear pet is likely to be most active at night while you are sleeping, it is important to make sure the cage suits it's needs. An ideal way to do this is to decorate it so that it simulates their natural environment. Include enough toys and opportunities for enrichment to keep your sugar glider occupied. The following tips will make your sugar glider's cage look and feel more natural and help your sugar gliders feel "at home" by encouraging consistency with their natural habitat:

- Consider using wood substrate as bedding for your sugar glider cage so it feels more natural.
- Incorporate plenty of branches (non-toxic wood) for perching and climbing.
- Include some eucalyptus branches, if you can find them, and replace them regularly as your sugar glider strips them of their leaves.
- Build or buy a nesting box that resembles a hollow log and texture the outside to make it good for climbing.
- Try feeding your sugar gliders at night, when they would naturally feed in the wild (instead of during the day).

- Offer live insects such as crickets to encourage your sugar gliders to "hunt" for their food.

c) Setting Up and Maintaining the Cage

Now you know the basics of what to include in your sugar glider cage you may be curious regarding how to set it up. One important aspect is the location of the cage, which should be easily accessible but not in a place where there will be considerable noise or traffic during the day while your sugar gliders are sleeping. The cage should be kept out of direct sunlight and in an area that is free from drafts. Sugar gliders prefer a temperature between 70°F and 90°F (21° to 32°C). Purchase a room thermometer to help monitor and maintain the correct temperature.

Not only do you need to provide an adequate cage for your sugar gliders, but you also have to keep it clean. Depending on the type of cage you decide on, cleaning may simply involve emptying and cleaning the tray beneath the cage that catches the waste, or to remove and replace any bedding you are using in the bottom of the cage. The more sugar gliders you have, the more frequently you will need to clean the cage, but you should expect to clean it at least once per week. In addition to replacing the bedding, clean and sanitize your sugar glider's food and water dishes and clean nesting materials.

How to: Schedule for Cleaning the Cage:

Daily:

- Clean and refill water bowls/bottle.
- Clean/sanitize food bowls.

Weekly:

- Remove and empty waste-collection tray.
- Clean and sanitize tray.
- Remove and replace litter (if using).
- Wash/sanitize nesting materials.

Monthly:

- Sanitize the entire cage.
- Wipe down the bars with pet-safe cleaning solution.
- Replace dirty/damaged nesting materials and accessories that cannot be cleaned.

Note: Though you will need to clean and sanitize your sugar glider's cage at least once per week, you should never have to bathe your sugar gliders themselves. Sugar gliders are naturally very clean animals and groom themselves. If your sugar glider stops grooming, it may be a sign of illness and you should seek immediate veterinary care.

2) *Feeding Sugar Gliders*

In the wild, sugar gliders tend to feed on a variety of insects and small invertebrates as well as fruit and sap from trees. In captivity, the diet of sugar gliders is very similar. To keep your sugar gliders happy and healthy, you must provide them with a well-balanced diet. In this section you will learn the basics about the nutritional needs of sugar gliders as well as tips for forming a healthy and balanced diet.

a) Nutritional Needs

Sugar gliders are omnivores. This means they require a mixture of vegetable-based and protein-based foods for proper nutrition. A correct sugar glider diet will consist of fruits, vegetables, meat and insects. To ensure your sugar gliders obtain the vitamins and minerals they need, it is recommended that you offer them small amounts of a commercial pellet specially formulated for sugar gliders on a daily basis.

Recommended brands of sugar glider pellets:
- Sunseed Vita Exotics Sugar Glider Formula.
- Pretty Pets Sugar Glider Food.

- Exotic Nutrition Glider Complete.
- Vitakraft Vita Smart Sugar Glider Food.
- Exotic Nutrition Instant-HPW Sugar Glider Diet.
- Quiko Sugar Glider Food.

b) Recommended Foods

A commercial sugar glider pellet should form what is known as your sugar glider's "staple diet", or in other words, the part of his diet that provides for his basic nutritional needs. Other foods you offer your sugar glider such as fruits, vegetables and insects, are part of his supplementary diet. To meet your sugar glider's basic nutritional needs, you should offer the following on a daily basis:

- 1 tablespoon commercial insectivore mix or live insects (see list on next page).
- 1 tablespoon commercial nectar mix.
- ½ to 1 teaspoon fresh vegetables.

As an alternative to a commercial nectar mix, you can offer your sugar glider Bourbon's modified Leadbeater's diet (BML), the recipe for which can be found in Appendix B at the back of this book. In regard to the insectivore mix, you should be offering a variety of zoo-quality insects for your sugar glider to enjoy such as:

- Crickets
- Meal worms
- Wax worms
- Moths
- Spiders

When feeding your sugar gliders live insects, always dust them with a multivitamin powder to ensure they receive enough calcium in their diet. Make sure to purchase human-grade supplements or formulas that are designed for sugar gliders and do not use reptile vitamin powder. In addition to supplements, provide your sugar glider with unlimited access to fresh water, favoring filtered or bottled water, not tap water. To increase your sugar glider's vitamin intake you can mix organic apple juice with his water a few times each week.

If you want to offer your sugar glider treats, good options include the following:

- Dried fruit (unsweetened)
- Dried vegetables
- Yogurt drops

- Fresh fruit
- Fresh vegetables

Note: It is incredibly important to maintain a balance of calcium and phosphorus in your sugar glider's diet. For this reason, you need to be diligent regarding overfeeding with fruits and vegetables. Only offer your sugar glider small amounts each time.

How to: Weekly Feeding Plan

Below you will find an example of a weekly feeding plan (Monday through to Friday) that you can use as a guide in structuring your sugar glider's diet. For simplicity, the amounts listed in the table are for one sugar glider and so will need to be adjusted accordingly to account for the actual number of gliders. For weekends you can simply repeat the diet from two of the weekdays.

Day	Time	Food	Amount
Monday	Morning	Insects	10-12 small, 7-10 medium
	Evening	BML mix (see Appendix B)	1 tablespoon
	Evening	Fresh apple	1 tablespoon

	Evening	Fresh corn	1 tablespoon
Tuesday	Morning	Unsalted, broiled chicken	1 teaspoon
	Evening	BML mix (see Appendix B)	1 tablespoon
	Evening	Fresh grapes	1 tablespoon
	Evening	Fresh carrots	1 tablespoon
	Evening	Neocalglucon (calcium supplement)	Tiny pinch
Wednesday	Morning	Insects	10-12 small, 7-10 medium
	Evening	BML mix (see Appendix B)	1 tablespoon
	Evening	Fresh melon	1 tablespoon
	Evening	Fresh peas	1 tablespoon
Thursday	Morning	Unsalted, boiled egg	1 teaspoon
	Evening	BML mix (see Appendix B)	1 tablespoon

	Evening	Fresh berries	1 tablespoon
	Evening	Fresh beans	1 tablespoon
	Evening	Nectar	Per directions
Friday	Morning	Insects	10-12 small, 7-10 medium
	Evening	BML mix (see Appendix B)	1 tablespoon
	Evening	Fresh melon	1 tablespoon
	Evening	Fresh peas	1 tablespoon

c) Foods to Avoid

As is true with any pet, there are certain foods that you should be avoided. Some foods are dangerous or toxic to sugar gliders and include:

- Chocolate
- Processed foods
- Fried foods
- Foods with artificial sweeteners
- Fruit pits and apple seeds
- Refined sugar
- High-fat foods
- Bread
- Dog or cat food

3) Sugar Glider Training and Behavior

Sugar gliders are very unique and interesting animals to keep as pets. Unlike a cat or a dog, you can carry your sugar glider around in your pocket all day and he will use you as something to climb on. Before you bring your sugar glider home you may want to familiarize yourself with some of the common sounds and behaviors these animals make which will help you form an understanding of your new pet. In this section you will learn about sugar glider behavior and valuable tips for handling and house training.

a) Common Sounds and Behaviors

The unique sounds and behaviors sugar gliders exhibit is one of the many reasons that make them interesting pets. Once your sugar glider is comfortable around you, it is not uncommon for your sugar gliders to try and groom you or run up the wall of the cage as you approach. Your sugar glider may also nibble or scrape his teeth along your skin. These behaviors are to be expected and part of a sugar glider's character.

It will take you some time to familiarize yourself with your sugar glider's behavior until you know what is and is not normal. However, meanwhile, you may find this list helpful:

Normal Sugar Glider Behaviors

- Hissing whilst defecating.
- Making barking noises.
- Nibbling on your hand.
- Taking food into a hiding place to eat.
- Sleeping in different places.
- Sneezing into hands then wiping face.
- Making "chitting" noises whilst playing with companions.
- Lunging at people passing the cage.
- Fretful by loud sounds/sudden movement.
- Tilting head before jumping/gliding.
- Sleeping on top of each other and forming a pile.

Abnormal Sugar Glider Behaviors

- Puffiness under the eyes.
- Dragging or favoring the hind legs.
- Eating their feces.
- Running in fast circles, frantic repetitive motions.

- Biting itself or over-grooming.
- Not eating or drinking.
- Failure to show interest in play.
- Rejecting or killing newborn joeys.

If you notice your sugar glider exhibiting any abnormal behaviors, it could be an indication of disease. In this case, it is wise to take your sugar glider to the vet as soon as possible.

In addition to interesting behaviors, sugar gliders also make some very unique sounds. Listed below are sugar glider sounds with an indication as to their likely meanings:

- **Crabbing** – sugar glider crabbing is a repeated screeching noise that indicates fear or agitation.
- **Barking** – sugar glider barking is a repeated loud barking sound, often exhibited at night (may be used to locate or warn other gliders, normal behavior) .
- **Hissing** – a common form of communication, typically a friendly behavior but may sometimes indicate desire to assert dominance.
- **Clicking** – used in close contact, often when the glider is investigating something new or potentially threatening.

- **Grunting** – a low, slow-paced repeated sound, often made when the sugar glider is experiencing pain or discomfort.
- **Shrieking** – often exhibited by nursing mothers when their nipples are tender and inflamed.
- **Singing** – a terse repeated sound often made by nursing mothers.
- **Sneezing** – often made when grooming, sugar gliders use mucus or saliva to work into their coats.
- **Popping** – a faint, subtle sound similar to a purr, often made when the sugar glider is content.

b) Handling and Interacting

Sugar gliders are very social animals and can form strong bonds with their owners and other household pets. This will not happen unless you spend plenty of time with your sugar glider. It is important to remember that sugar gliders are wild animals, so unless they acquire plenty of handling by humans, they will not completely tame. It is a good idea to give your sugar glider a day or two to acclimatize to his new surroundings when you first bring him home, after that you will need to socialize him and get him used to being handled.

When you first start hand training your sugar glider it is a good idea to do it in a closed room. Place your sugar glider in a hanging pouch around your neck so he has somewhere to retreat to if he becomes frightened. Carefully remove your sugar glider from the pouch and allow him to crawl around in your hands and along your arms and shoulders. If your sugar glider jumps off your body, don't be alarmed, simply pick him up and place him back on your arm each time it happens. The more you handle your sugar glider, the more used to you he will get and before you know it he will be content to sleep in your lap. To answer the frequently asked question, "do sugar gliders bite?" – yes, you shouldn't be surprised if your sugar glider nips you from time to time, especially while you are working at taming him.

c) House Training Sugar Gliders

You cannot house train a sugar glider as you would a dog or litter train him in the way you would a cat. You can, however, predict when your sugar glider will have to relieve himself, therefore giving him the opportunity to do so in a place that will not make a mess in his cage or on your clothes. Sugar gliders are very predictable and will need to eliminate waste after waking up from a nap, within 15 minutes of a meal and about every 3 to 4 hours in between. You should be able to predict when your sugar glider will need to go to the toilet and place him on a tissue or paper towel and dispose of it after completion.

You will be glad to know that sugar gliders have a natural aversion to soiling their beds. This makes it easier to clean nesting boxes and also means that they are unlikely to have an "accident" in your clothes unless they are unable to get out. If you plan to spend time with your sugar gliders at night when they are most active, give them a few minutes to do their business after waking up before you handle them.

d) Bonding with Your Sugar Glider

As you are already aware, sugar gliders are wild animals and so will not automatically be tame when you bring them home. When you purchase a baby sugar glider from a breeder, you may hear the term "hand tame." There are different definitions for this name, so you may want to ask the breeder to clarify it's meaning. In some cases, hand tame simply means that the sugar glider will accept food from humans, while in other cases it may mean that the sugar glider will sit calmly in your hand.

Bonding with your sugar glider is a process that can take some time to achieve, so be patient, When you first bring your sugar glider home, drape a piece of worn clothing over the cage so he becomes accustomed to your scent. During the first two or three days at home, do not remove your sugar gliders from the cage or try to handle them, instead, feed them as you normally would and sit in the room with them, talking to them if you wish. During this time you can also offer your sugar gliders small treats through the cage such as yogurt drops.

After the first few days you can begin to carry your glider around in a pouch so he can familiarize himself around you. The pouches used to enable your sugar glider to spend time and connect with you are typically called sugar glider bonding pouches. Start by taking your sugar glider from the cage during the day when he is still sleepy and place him in the pouch. As you carry your glider around, talk to him softly with a calm tone. You can also offer yogurt drops or other treats to encourage your sugar glider. When you are able to place your hand into the cage or into the pouch without being bitten or without your sugar glider crabbing at you, you are ready to move to the next stage.

To encourage and distract your sugar glider, try dipping your finger into yogurt and allowing him a few licks. Once your sugar glider is calm, try to pet him gently. When you are able to do so without him crabbing at you, progress to placing your hand under his body so that he is sitting in your hand. Continue to use yogurt as a treat and a distraction to keep your sugar glider from biting you. You may also want to position your fingers so that your sugar glider has something to hold on to.

Once your sugar glider has learned to sit calmly in your hand you can now start the true bonding process. Take your glider out of the cage while he is sleeping and make a point of carrying him around in a sugar glider bonding pouch with you during the day. Keep the pouch zipped but spend several hours each day with your glider. After a week or so, you can start to leave the pouch unzipped to see if your sugar glider will come out to explore. If your sugar glider does come out, make sure he stays with you, if he jumps down just scoop him back up.

After you and your glider have bonded you can start to play games with him, which will increase the bond and develop his intelligence. Try using a feather or a string to give your glider something to chase. Keep plenty of treats on hand during playtime and make sure you do not reward the glider if he nips your fingers. Be sure your playtime is in a glider-proofed room for the safety of your pet. If you haven't already, the time you spend bonding with your sugar glider is a perfect opportunity to think of sugar glider names.

Chapter Six: Breeding Sugar Gliders

Breeding sugar gliders is not something you should do on impulse - it will take a lot of experience and knowledge to be able to breed sugar gliders safely and correctly. If you are considering breeding your sugar gliders to make a little extra money, think again. Not only are you unlikely to make a profit after you take into account veterinary costs for potential complications and the cost of raising the joeys, but there is also the expense of licensing yourself as a breeder. If however you feel up to the challenge of breeding your sugar gliders, you will find some valuable information in this chapter giving you have an idea what to expect from sugar glider breeding.

1) Basic Breeding Information

Before you can breed your sugar gliders there are many steps you need to take. Firstly you will need to familiarize yourself with the reproductive process of sugar gliders – at what age they reach sexual maturity, when they can be safely bred and the timetable for conception, gestation and birth. You will also need to take extreme caution in selecting your sugar gliders for breeding. Making the mistake of breeding sugar gliders that are closely related, could produce genetic defects in the joeys.

Sugar gliders typically breed once per year in the wild, but if the climate is right and food is abundant, they may breed more often. In captivity however, sugar gliders can breed at any time of year. In regard to litter size, two is the most common number of Joeys born in a litter, though there are cases where only one Joey is born. After a 14 to 16-day gestation period, the tiny Joey is born and makes the climb up the mother's belly into her pouch. There the Joey will latch itself onto the nipple and stay attached for at least 40 days.

About 60 to 70 days after the Joey enters the pouch, he will emerge and start to live in the nest. Joeys typically live in the nest until they are about 110 to 111 days old, although they may be fully weaned from their mother by the age of 2 months. It isn't until they reach 7 to 10 months of age that joeys become fully independent and able to live on their own. It is also around this time when they start to become sexually mature and capable of breeding. Therefore it is essential that you separate male joeys from their mother and opposite sex joeys from each other to prevent interbreeding.

Below you will find an overview of information about the breeding process for sugar gliders:

- Typically breed once or twice a year in the wild.
- Breeding frequency depends on climate and availability of food.
- May breed more frequently in captivity.
- Breeding season in the wild is continuous but peaks between June and November.
- The number of joeys born is 1 to 2, (2 most common).
- Gestation period for females lasts 16 days.
- After 16 days, joeys climb up the mother's belly into the pouch and attach to the nipple.
- Joeys remain attached to the nipple for 40 days.

- Young joeys emerge from the pouch after 60 to 70 days.
- At birth, joeys have no fur and their eyes are closed.
- The eyes open about 12 to 14 days after the Joey leaves the pouch.
- Joeys continue to live in the nest after emerging from the pouch until approx 111 days old.
- Weaning occurs by 2 months of age.
- Joeys become independent between 7 and 10 months.
- Sexual maturity in males develops at 8 to 15 months.
- Sexual maturity in females develops around 12 months of age.

a) Selecting Sugar Gliders for Breeding

Following understanding of the basics regarding the breeding process of sugar gliders, you can learn the specifics about how to select a breeding pair. You cannot simply breed any female sugar glider to any male, you need to acquire a record of their lineage to ensure that they are not related within at least 4 to 5 generations. In order to breed your sugar gliders properly, you will need to obtain them from a reputable breeder who has records of his own sugar gliders' lineage.

2) *The Breeding Process*

Female sugar gliders reach sexual maturity anywhere between 8 and 15 months of age. For the safety of your females however, you should err on the side of caution and avoid breeding until they are at least 10 to 12 months old. If you breed your female sugar gliders too young, you run the risk of complications and rejection of the Joey by the female. It is also unwise to breed a sugar glider that is still growing and developing as pregnancy will put a great deal of stress on her body and may deprive the expectant mother of nutrients she will need for her own health.

A female sugar glider has an estrus cycle lasting around 28 days and ovulation occurs approx 2 days after the onset of the cycle. When a female sugar glider is in season, she will likely become a little more agitated than usual and may make a calling sound to her mate. If you plan to breed your sugar gliders, you will need to introduce the male and female while the female is in season, and mating should occur within 24 hours.

During mating, sugar gliders are unlikely to show any interest in food and they may exhibit changes in behavior.

Male sugar gliders for example, will climb onto the female and may even bite her neck during mating. In most cases these bites are superficial, but if the skin is broken, you should seek veterinary care for your female sugar glider as soon as possible to prevent infection. If conception occurs, the female will go through a 14 to 16-day gestation period before the Joey is born to climb up her belly into her pouch, attach itself to the nipple and develop for the next 60 to 70 days.

After about 30 days, the Joey will have grown large enough to produce a visible bulge in the female's abdomen. When the Joey is a week or so away from emerging from the pouch, you may even see parts protruding from the pouch - a leg, tail or maybe an arm. During the period when the Joey is nursing, it is important that you provide your female sugar glider with a healthy diet. She will need extra food (especially protein) to help her produce enough milk to support the joeys. If an adequate diet is not provided, you run the risk of the female cannibalizing the joeys.

3) Raising the Joeys

About 10 weeks after the Joey is born, they will emerge from the pouch. It is not uncommon for the Joey to remain attached to the nipple for another day or two after emerging from the pouch, so be very careful in handling your sugar glider to prevent the Joey from detaching prematurely. Once the Joey has completely left the pouch he will likely cling to his mother and spend most of his time nursing. He may even go in and out of the pouch for the next week or so until he is too large to fit anymore.

Once the Joey emerges from the pouch completely, the father will start to play an important role in his care. When the Joey is still small, he will be unable to generate his own body heat so he will rely on the father to keep him warm in the nest when his mother leaves to eat. As soon as the Joey emerges from the pouch, you should remove all but one of the nesting areas from the cage so the parents have only one option. The father may care for the Joey for the next several weeks until it starts to wander outside of the nest of his own accord.

As the Joey develops you will need to take steps to socialize him and get him used to being handled by humans. Start as soon as the Joey emerges from the pouch, handling him for just a few minutes each day whilst the mother is out of the nest eating or playing. By the time the Joey is two weeks old, its eyes should have opened and it will start to grow fur. At this time the parents will begin to leave the Joey alone for longer periods, this will enable you to extend the amount of time you spend handling him.

Once the Joey reaches 5 weeks of age, the weaning process will begin. As the Joey is weaned, you will notice his tail become fluffier and his fur will start to thicken. By the time he is 8 to 10 weeks old he should be fully weaned and ready to be separated from the parents. If you are planning to sell your joeys, do not do so until they are at least 8 weeks old and fully weaned.

a) Caring for a Rejected Joey

There are a number of reasons why a female sugar glider may reject her Joey, but it is most common in cases when the female sugar glider is bred too young. In the event that your female sugar glider abandons her Joey, you need to take quick action to save him. The first step is recognizing when a Joey has been abandoned. Sugar glider parents will leave the Joey alone for short periods of time to eat and play, but there is a difference between temporarily leaving the Joey and abandoning him. Below you will find a list of signs, which indicate a Joey has been abandoned:

- The Joey is left alone for more than 10 to 15 minutes at any one time by both parents.
- Neither parent responds when the Joey cries for a long time.
- The Joey tries to crawl out of the nest too early – before 4 weeks out of the pouch.
- The Joey is found alone and cold in a different nesting area from the parents.
- Joey is found with bite or scratch marks on him.
- Mother repeatedly pushes the Joey away when he tries to nurse.

If you suspect that the Joey has been abandoned, your first move is to check for dehydration. To do so, gently pull up the skin above the Joey's shoulder blades. If it sticks up or stays 'tented', the Joey is dehydrated. In cases of severe dehydration, take the Joey to the vet for emergency treatment. If the Joey is only slightly dehydrated you can give him small amounts of Pedialyte every hour over the next 6 hours or so.

Once the Joey has been rehydrated you will need to begin a feeding regimen. To feed the Joey you will need to use a small needle-less syringe. Begin by wrapping the Joey in a warm cloth and hold him so his head is up and tail down, parallel to the wall. Use the syringe to apply droplets of formula to the Joey's lips one drop at a time – never force the formula into the Joey's mouth or he could choke. Follow the recommendations below regarding what to feed the Joey, bearing in mind that you will need to make the transition onto replacement formula slowly to prevent bloating.

Day 1: 75% Pedialyte, 25% replacement formula
Day 2: 50% Pedialyte, 50% replacement formula
Day 3: 25% Pedialyte, 75% replacement formula
Day 4: 100% replacement formula

Chapter Seven: Maintaining Sugar Glider Health

Sugar gliders are naturally very healthy and as long as you provide them with a clean environment and balanced diet, are likely to stay that way. Unlike dogs and cats, these pets do not typically require frequent veterinary care. However this doesn't mean that you should take your sugar glider's health for granted, you should still take the time to learn about diseases that could potentially affect your sugar glider so you know how to manage them. In this chapter you will learn about common health and hygiene problems for sugar gliders as well as tips for preventing illness and selecting a vet.

1) Common Health and Hygiene Problems

As you have already read, sugar gliders are very healthy animals by nature. You do not need to have your sugar glider vaccinated against any particular disease, and as long as you keep his cage clean and his diet balanced, you hopefully shouldn't have any problem with illnesses. However, it is always wise to be prepared. To ensure that you are able to diagnose and treat sugar glider diseases when they occur, you would do well to familiarize yourself with some health problems commonly seen in this species. In this section you will receive an overview of the most common conditions affecting sugar gliders including the causes, symptoms and treatment options.

Diseases and conditions covered in this section include:
- Actinomycosis
- Depression
- Diarrhea
- Giardiasis
- Hind Leg Paralysis
- Metabolic Bone Disease
- Mites and Fleas
- Polioencephalomalacia

Actinomycosis

Also known as lumpy jaw, this disease is caused by the bacteria *Actinomyces israeli*. This disease manifests in the form of a hard, slowly growing lump in the face or neck area. If untreated, this condition can progress quickly and lead to infections of the lung, intestines and other parts of the body. Without treatment, actinomycosis can eventually become fatal.

In addition to the development of a lump, other symptoms of actinomycosis include weight loss and eye discharge. This condition is the result of facial tissues coming into contact with the bacteria, often through trauma or surgery. In sugar gliders in particular, dental abscesses are a common cause. In most cases prescription medication is required to eradicate the infection, so you should seek veterinary care immediately for your sugar glider if you suspect actinomycosis.

Depression

When you think of diseases likely to affect your pets, depression may not be the first thing that springs to mind. Because sugar gliders are such social animals, they are likely to develop symptoms of depression if they do not receive adequate attention from their owners. Disease and the loss of a companion animal are also factors that may contribute to depression in sugar gliders.

Some symptoms you are likely to notice if your sugar glider becomes depressed include a lack of interest in toys, decreased desire to play, lethargy or inactivity, change in sleeping habits and excessive noise making. Treatment for depression in sugar gliders simply involves spending more time with your pet and perhaps getting him a companion. Routinely changing his toys may also help to keep him mentally stimulated.

Preventing depression in sugar gliders is fairly easy, simply provide numerous and varied toys and plenty of playtime. Having more than one sugar glider is also beneficial in preventing depression and making sure your sugar glider's cage is large enough to accommodate play.

Diarrhea

When your sugar glider is healthy his stools should appear as small, hard pellets that look very similar to mouse droppings. If your sugar glider's stools start to become mushy or liquid or if he begins to defecate excessively, it could be an indication of a very severe problem. If diarrhea is left untreated, it could result in a dangerous loss of fluids and dehydration in your pet.

Some common causes of diarrhea include bacterial or viral infections, stress, parasite infections, bowel disease, or a reaction to certain foods (such as dairy). If your sugar glider has diarrhea, you can feed him small amounts of Pedialyte to restore his electrolytes and prevent dehydration. You should, however, consult a veterinarian to help determine the cause of his diarrhea and to determine the exact treatment. The underlying causes of diarrhea (such as infection) can easily be prevented by providing your sugar glider with a healthy diet and by keeping his cage clean, therefore avoiding contact with harmful pathogens such as bacterial and viruses.

Giardiasis

Also referred to as a Giardia bloom, giardiasis is caused by microscopic parasites that invade the intestinal tract. These parasites can remain in your sugar glider's intestinal tract for extended periods of time before any symptoms are disclosed. During this time, the parasites can reproduce rapidly. The most common symptom of a giardia infection is diarrhea. Other signs may include change in behavior, vomiting, jaundice, green stools and dehydration.

Giardiasis is caused by the Giardia parasite to which your sugar gliders may be exposed to by coming into contact with stools from an infected animal. Another potential cause for giardia levels to grow out of control in the intestines is stress – extreme stress can also lead to other digestive problems in sugar gliders.

The first step in treating this disease is to quarantine the sick and infected sugar glider. Clean and sterilize the cage thoroughly to ensure the infection does not spread. Always wash your hands before and after handling your gliders and before preparing their food. If the condition doesn't improve, seek veterinary care.

Hind Leg Paralysis

Hind leg paralysis is commonly caused by inadequate levels of calcium in your sugar glider. This condition is very dangerous and if not treated correctly can become fatal. If detected in time however, the condition is completely reversible. Because this condition is caused by an imbalance of calcium, it is easily preventable by providing your sugar gliders with a healthy and well-balanced diet.

Signs and symptoms of this disease include lethargy, limping, tremors, weakness, inability to walk and paralysis of the hind limbs. In addition to giving your sugar glider a healthy diet, you should also seek veterinary care if your pet exhibits any symptoms of this condition. In extreme cases, your veterinarian may recommend supplementation, but generally the problem can be solved with the sugar glider's diet, which can be sufficient to reverse the condition.

Metabolic Bone Disease

Also known by the name nutritional osteodystrophy, metabolic bone disease is the result of an imbalance of minerals in the body. When your sugar glider's diet doesn't contain an adequate balance of calcium and phosphorus, among other minerals, it is likely to cause a number of problems. Common symptoms of this condition include weakening of the leg muscles and paralysis of the hind legs. This condition can also lead to pneumonia, seizures, heart problems and bone fractures or breaks.

As long as this condition is diagnosed and treated quickly, the damage can generally be reversed. Treatment basically involves cage rest and supplementation with calcium and vitamin D_3, which can be given in injection form by your veterinarian. Correcting your sugar glider's diet is also very important for the treatment and prevention of this disease. One way to ensure your sugar glider has adequate calcium, is by dusting feeder insects with calcium powder prior to feeding him.

Mites and Fleas

In the wild it is fairly common for sugar gliders to come into contact with mites, fleas and other insect parasites. In captivity however, the risk is much lower. If you have other pets such as cats and dogs, your sugar gliders may be at risk of contracting them. If your sugar gliders do catch mites or fleas, the best course of action is to dust them with an insecticide recommended by your veterinarian. You will also need to thoroughly clean and sanitize the nesting materials in your sugar glider's cage to prevent re-infestation.

If you do have other pets at home, it is very important that you also treat them to prevent or eradicate fleas and mites. A monthly topical preventive is generally adequate to prevent your other pets from developing flea and mite infestations that may be passed on to your sugar gliders.

Polioencephalomalacia

This condition is a type of neurological disease that leads to deterioration in certain parts of the brain. The exact cause of this condition is largely unknown, but it is thought that certain nutritional deficiencies may play a role in its development. Treatment with vitamin B1 (thiamine) supplements has shown a noticeable improvement in affected sugar gliders, so it is reasonable to assume that nutritional deficiencies are related to the cause of the disease or at least making it worse.

Some symptoms of polioencephalomalacia include weakness, dizziness, lacking in energy, loss of coordination, weight loss and change in appetite. Sugar gliders with this condition may also develop tremors and eventual paralysis. Because the exact cause of this condition is unknown, preventive measures are at best, guesswork. Feeding your sugar gliders a healthy, well-balanced diet will certainly help to prevent this and other diseases.

2) Preventing Illness

The key for keeping your sugar gliders happy and healthy is to provide them with a clean and suitable environment along with a nutritious diet, and with proper care, generally sugar gliders will not require frequent veterinary care. In order to ensure that your sugar gliders remain healthy, it would be wise to familiarize yourself with some common problems and advice for prevention. There are several conditions that can affect sugar gliders which are not related to disease but nevertheless be the result of exposure to toxic substances or inadequate diet. In most cases these problems are easily preventable.

In this section you will learn some helpful tips for preventing common problems with sugar gliders including the following:

- Aflatoxicosis
- Nutritional Deficiencies
- Constipation
- Toxicity Poisoning
- Dehydration
- Stress

Aflatoxicosis

This is a condition that will result from feeding your sugar gliders food that has been contaminated with toxins that are produced by certain fungi. Foods most likely to be contaminated include corn, peanuts and cottonseed. Your sugar gliders may also be affected if they eat crickets that have been fed contaminated feed. Some indications of aflatoxicosis include loss of appetite, fatigue, diarrhea, anaemia and jaundice. If a diagnosis is detected early, this condition is very treatable. However, the easiest way to prevent it is to avoid feeding your sugar glider peanuts and corn and to make sure all food is clean.

Nutritional Deficiencies

One of the most common nutritional deficiencies seen in sugar gliders (and one of the most preventable) is calcium deficiency. This condition results not only from inadequate levels of calcium in their diet, but also from an imbalance of calcium, phosphorus and vitamin D. This condition can be prevented by providing a well balanced diet. Another nutritional deficiency easily prevented is hypoproteinemia or anaemia, resulting from inadequate protein in their diet. To ensure that your sugar glider doesn't suffer from any nutritional deficiencies, you may want to consider including pellet food specially formulated for sugar gliders as part of their diet. Insects such as crickets and mealworms are also a good source of protein.

Constipation

Constipation is another problem often caused by poor nutrition. Not only is this condition uncomfortable and painful for your sugar gliders, it can lead to some very dangerous complications. The key to preventing constipation is to provide plenty of fresh water and a diet high in fiber. Ensuring that your sugar glider receives plenty of exercise will also help prevent constipation.

Toxicity Poisoning

Sugar gliders are very active and curious creatures, so it is important that you proof your home before bringing in your new pets. Even seemingly innocuous items such as houseplants can be potential sources of poison for your sugar gliders. It is essential that you keep all food containers tightly closed, chemicals and cleaning products are stored out of your gliders' reach and you do not allow your glider to eat your other pets' food.

Dehydration

Dehydration is very dangerous for sugar gliders, but very easy to prevent. You should always provide your sugar glider with unlimited access of fresh water, you may even want to provide a shallow dish of water in addition to their bottle. Some symptoms of dehydration in sugar gliders include vomiting, diarrhea, seizures, dry nose and mouth, reduced frequency of urination, difficult bowel movements, lethargy and rapid breathing. If you suspect your sugar glider is suffering from dehydration you should contact a veterinarian immediately.

a) Recognizing and Treating Stress in Sugar Gliders

As much as you try to provide for your sugar glider's every need, you still have to be watchful for signs of stress. Obviously your sugar gliders are unable to communicate verbally when they are not feeling well or something is wrong, so you need to learn to recognize the signs of stress. If your sugar glider becomes chronically stressed over a long period of time, it can have devastating effects on his health. He may stop playing, refuse to eat and could most likely to get sick. There are a number of reasons that can cause stress in sugar gliders including the following:

- Moving into a new home or a new cage.
- Travelling (either a short journey to the vet or a longer journey e.g. vacation).
- Losing a cage mate or gaining a new one.
- Weaning a Joey (applies to pregnant females).
- Change in diet or routine.
- Loneliness, boredom or lack of attention.
- Illness or injury that is left untreated.

Your sugar gliders may display signs of stress in different ways, and may not always be obvious. The key to recognizing the symptoms of stress is to become familiar with your sugar glider's usual behavior so you are more likely to notice if something changes. Some possible signs of stress in sugar gliders include:

- **Irritability or unusual aggression** – your glider may exhibit a fighting stance, lunge at you, or bite you.
- **Barking or crying** – these signs are often related to loneliness and a need for attention.
- **Eating fecal matter** – the term for this condition is "coprophagia" and is often exhibited by sugar gliders when they are stressed due to a poor diet.
- **Changes in eating habits** – stops eating or starts eating much more than usual, could be a signs of stress.
- **Pacing and repetitive behaviors** – some gliders exhibit these behaviors anyway, but if it is unusual for your glider, it could be stress related.
- **Self-mutilating or over grooming** – when sugar gliders become stressed they are prone to over grooming that may result in patches of thinning fur.
- **Lethargy or inactivity** – sugar gliders are naturally very active, so if yours become lethargic, it may mean something is wrong.

The key to dealing with your sugar glider's stress is to identify the cause and then remedy it. If your sugar glider is unhappy with his diet, make a change. If he is lonely or bored, give him new toys and make an effort to afford him more time and attention throughout the day. The sooner you deal with your sugar glider's stress, the more likely he is to make a full recovery.

3) Sugar Glider First Aid

Sugar gliders are very active and playful creatures, so they are at times prone to minor injuries. If you are not careful regarding the kind of toys and type of materials you use in your sugar glider's cage, his claws could get caught, which may lead to broken toes or worse, broken limbs. It is also possible for your sugar glider to get minor cuts and scratches during play with cage mates. In the event that your sugar glider does develop a minor injury, it is wise to know how to handle the situation. Sugar glider first aid can be tricky, but if the time comes when you have to use it, you will be glad you know how.

a) Compiling a First Aid Kit

Because you will never be able to predict what injury your sugar gliders may sustain, it's a good idea to keep a fully stocked first aid kit to hand. Below you will find a list of items to include in your first aid kit as well as a brief explanation as to what they can be used for:

- Shot-glass e-collar - a collar used to prevent the sugar glider from causing further injury to itself.
- Large straws - to cover the tail.

- Sterile saline wash – for cleaning wounds.
- Alcohol wipes - for hand sanitation.
- Baby wipes, fragrance free - for cleaning fur.
- Antiseptic ointment - for treating minor wounds.
- Cotton swaps - for cleaning wounds, applying medication.
- Sterile gauze pads - for covering wounds.
- Adhesive tape – to secure gauze, e-collar, etc.
- Styptic powder - to stop bleeding.
- Side-edge cut clippers - for nail trimming.
- Sterile slip tip syringes - for medication administration or oral feeding.
- Baby food - for emergency feeding.
- Pedialyte - for emergency hydration.
- Hand warmer for necessary travelling.
- Instant ice pack for necessary travelling.
- Small Popsicle sticks - for splinting breaks.
- Tweezers.
- Tissues/towels.
- Emergency vet information.
- Gliders veterinary records.
- Copy of permit/license.

b) First Aid Procedures

If your glider has a minor wound such as a cut or scratch, you can handle it the same way as for a human. Clean the wound with sterile saline solution and apply an antiseptic ointment before covering with clean gauze. You may also need to fit your glider with an e-collar to prevent him from removing the gauze and re-injuring himself. For injuries that involve significant blood loss or broken bones, get your sugar glider to an emergency vet as soon as possible.

The aftermath of an injury may require you to provide your sugar glider with special care at home. You may for instance, have to administer oral medication using a needle-less syringe. Following the steps below will guide you safely through the administering of oral medication to your sugar gliders:

1. Fill your needle-less syringe with the appropriate dosage and set it aside within easy reach.

2. Carefully wrap your sugar glider in a towel and lay him on his back so his mouth is easily accessible.

3. Place one hand on the sugar glider's collarbone to hold him still while you pick up the syringe with the other hand.

4. Insert the tip of the syringe into the side of your glider's mouth, pushing it as far back as possible over the top of the tongue.

5. Depress the plunger on the syringe, making sure the medication enters the back of the glider's mouth and down his throat, rather than leaking out the sides of his mouth.

6. Do not allow your glider to shake his head afterwards - continue to hold him firmly but gently until he swallows.

7. To encourage your glider to swallow, rub the tip of his nose with your finger – he will lick his nose and swallow.

8. Reward your glider with a yogurt drop or mealworm to help clear the taste of the medicine from his mouth.

c) Procedures to Avoid

Certain injuries can be taken care of by you, such as the treating of minor wounds, but others should only be carried out by a professional veterinarian. Below you will find a list of procedures that should only be performed by a vet or should not be performed at all:

1. **Clipping the teeth** – unlike some pets (such as guinea pigs), a sugar glider's teeth will not grow back if clipped.

2. **Suturing the cloaca** – if you suture or damage the cloaca, your sugar glider will be unable to urinate or defecate and the damage could be irreparable.

3. **Using pain relieving ointment without an e-collar** – if you use any kind of ointment on your sugar glider, you will need to fit an e-collar to prevent him from licking it off - pain relieving ointment may numb your sugar glider's tongue and therefore bite himself without realizing.

4. **Do not use Metacam for more than 5 days** – Metacam is a popular pain relief used for sugar

gliders, and if taken for long periods, can lead to liver problems.

d) Setting up a Hospital Cage

If your sugar glider is injured or is sick and you need to avoid spreading disease to other gliders, you may have to isolate him. Setting up an isolation or hospital cage for sugar gliders is fairly easy and is always a good idea to have one to hand in case it's needed. Follow the steps below to set up your hospital cage:

- Choose a small cage to use as a hospital cage – a sire cage or a 38-gallon vivarium will suffice.

- If your sugar glider needs to be separated for a long period of time, choose something larger such as a 65 gallon vivarium.

- Make adaptations to the cage to allow sugar gliders wearing e-collars to access food and water:

  o Place a large pouch (to use as a nest box) in the corner of the cage and use a large clip to hold it open.

- o Install a horizontal hammock across the cage, approx halfway up, to act as a safety net in case your sugar glider falls.

- o Use bird-style feeders to contain their food - they will have difficulty eating from bowls whilst wearing an e-collar.

- Install a small exercise wheel in the cage enabling your glider to run, without the wheel taking up too much space.

- For gliders with mobility issues, consider tilting food and water dishes for easier access.

- Be creative in designing your sugar glider's hospital cage so that it suits his individual needs during his recovery.

4) Veterinary Care for Sugar Gliders

Although sugar gliders are generally very healthy, it is always a good idea to have the contact details to hand of a local veterinarian that you can call if you have an issue. Bear in mind that sugar gliders are exotic pets, so you cannot simply take them to a regular vet, but will need to locate a vet that is experienced and licensed, to care for exotic pets like the sugar glider. Because sugar gliders have been domesticated for more than 15 years and are increasing in popularity as pets, it shouldn't be too difficult to find one in your area.

In order to find a veterinarian who is experienced with sugar gliders, you can conduct an online search or ask a local vet for recommendations. An alternative option is to use a veterinarian database such as this one:

Exotic Nutrition

www.exoticnutrition.com

Once you have found a veterinarian whose expertise include treating sugar gliders, you should take the time to ask a few questions to ensure they are truly experienced. Some of the questions you could ask may include:

- How many sugar gliders have you treated and how long have you been involved with them?

- Do you consult with other experienced sugar glider veterinarians when needed?

- What is included in a standard check-up?

- Do you offer additional services such as trimming nails?

- What kind of neutering procedures do you use?

- Are you available after hours for emergencies?

You may also like to ask for referrals from other sugar glider owners to make sure the vet offers quality service. It can also be very useful to be in contact with other sugar glider owners to exchange information and advice.

Chapter Eight: Sugar Gliders Care Sheet

In reading this book you have received a great deal of information about keeping sugar gliders as pets, from purchasing sugar gliders to preparing their cage and how to care for them. Immediately after bringing your sugar glider home, you may have questions that require a quick and simple answer. Rather than having to leaf through the entire book to find the answer, refer to this care sheet. Here you will find all the basic information about sugar gliders including a cage set-up guide, nutritional and breeding information.

1) Basic Information

- Scientific name is *Petaurus breviceps.*
- Belongs to marsupial infraclass.
- Related to various gliding possum species.
- Arboreal and nocturnal by nature.
- Has large eyes, swivel ears, prehensile tail, syndactylous toes, patagium.
- Fur is soft and thick.
- Color is blue-grey, paling to cream on the chest and throat.
- Typical markings include a black stripe from nose halfway down the back.
- Color variations may include yellow, tan or albino (very rare).
- Average body length is 5 to 6 inches (12.7 to 15.2cm).
- Average tail length is 7 to 8 inches (17.8 to 20.3cm).
- Average weight for males is 4 to 5.6 oz. (115 to 160g).
- Average weight for females is 3.3 to 4.75 oz. (95 to 135g).
- The average sugar glider life expectancy is up to 9 years in the wild, up to 12 years in captivity.
- Diet in the wild consists of insects, small vertebrates, fruit and tree sap.

2) Cage Set-up Guide

- The minimum cage dimensions for a sugar glider are 24 x 24 x 36 inches (61 x 61 x 91.4cm).
- The height of the cage is very important so sugar gliders can jump and climb.
- The best cage materials are metal wire or wire mesh to allow climbing.
- Metal cages should have horizontal, not vertical bars.
- The maximum spacing between bars should be 1/2 inch (1.27cm).
- For solid-based cages, use pine shavings to absorb urine.
- Cages with a mesh base allow droppings to fall through into a collection tray.
- Necessary cage supplies include food bowl, water bottle, exercise wheel and nesting box.
- Consider fabric nesting materials because they are easy to wash.
- Provide ladders, ropes and plenty of toys such as bird toys etc.
- Simulate a natural environment using branches, hollow tree nests and wood bedding.

- The ideal temperature for a sugar glider cage is between 70°F and 90°F (21° to 32°C).
- The cage should be placed in a location that is accessible but not too noisy during the day.
- Clean food/water bowls daily.
- Remove and replace litter (or clean collection tray) at least once a week.

3) Nutritional Information

- Sugar gliders are omnivorous - they eat insects, small invertebrates, fruit and sap.
- A well-balanced sugar glider diet is required to meet their nutritional needs.
- Commercial (or homemade) pellet food is recommended as a staple diet.
- Consider using a commercial insectivore mix along with live insects.
- Commercial nectar mixes can help to balance your sugar glider's nutrition.
- Insects enjoyed by sugar gliders include crickets, mealworms, wax worms, moths, spiders and more.
- Fresh water should be supplied at all times (use bottled, not tap water).
- Treats for sugar gliders include dried fruit, dried and fresh vegetables, yogurt drops and fresh fruit.
- Avoid chocolate, processed food, fried food, artificial sweeteners, fruit pits/seeds and refined sugar.

4) Breeding Information

- Typically breed once or twice a year in the wild.
- Breeding frequency depends on climate and availability of food.
- May breed more frequently in captivity.
- Breeding season in the wild is continuous but peaks between June and November.
- The average litter size is 1 to 2 joeys, with 2 being the most common.
- Gestation period for females lasts 16 days.
- After 16 days, joeys climb up the mother's belly into the pouch and attach itself to the nipple.
- Joeys remain attached to the nipple for about 40 days.
- Young joeys emerge from the pouch after 60 to 70 days.
- At birth joeys have no fur and closed eyes.
- The eyes open about 12 to 14 days after the Joey leaves the pouch.
- Joeys continue to live in the nest after emerging from the pouch until approx 111 days old.
- Weaning occurs by 2 months of age.

- Joeys become independent between 7 and 10 months.
- Sexual maturity in males develops at 8 to 15 months.
- Sexual maturity in females develops around 12 months.

Appendix A: Relevant Websites

Throughout this book you have received substantial information relating to keeping and caring for sugar gliders as pets. There may come a time however, when you need additional information or resources regarding a certain subject. Should this need arise, refer to the relevant websites in this chapter for guidance. Here you will find resources for sugar glider food, supplies, licensing information and even pet insurance websites.

1) *Food and Supplies for Sugar Gliders*

United States Websites:

SugarGlider.com.
www.sugarglider.com

Doctors Foster and Smith.
www.drsfostersmith.com

"Sugar Glider Foods." Exotic Nutrition.
www.exoticnutrition.com/suglfo

"Sugar Glider Toys." Suncoast Sugar Gliders.
www.sugar-gliders.com/glider-toys-list

United Kingdom Websites:

"Sugar Glider Food and Supplements."
"Sugar Glider Pouches & Cage Accessories."
Sugar Glider Shop.
www.sugarglidershop.co.uk

"Guide to Keeping Sugar Gliders." Holly House Veterinary Hospital.

www.hollyhousevets.co.uk/exotics/sugar-gliders

"Wodent Exercise Wheel." PetPlanet.co.uk.

www.petplanet.co.uk

2) *Cages for Sugar Gliders*

United States Websites:

"Sugar Glider Cages." Exotic Nutrition.
www.exoticnutrition.com/suglca

"Cages, Habitats and Hutches." PetSmart.com.
www.petsmart.com

"Sugar Glider Cages." The Sugar Glider Superstore.
www.sugar-glider-store.com/cages

"Cage Setup." Pocket Pets.
www.sugargliderinfo.org

United Kingdom Websites:

"Sugar Glider Cages." PetCagesUK.
www.petcagesuk.co.uk/sugar-glider-cages

"DIY Sugar Glider Cage." eHow.co.uk.
www.ehow.co.uk/how_8450947_diy-sugar-glider-cage

"Multi Storey Cages." ZooPlus.co.uk.

www.zooplus.co.uk

"Sugar Glider Cages." BonanzaMarket.co.uk.

www.bonanzamarket.co.uk

3) Licensing and Purchase Info for Sugar Gliders

United States Websites:

APHIS Animal Transport Permit.
www.aphis.usda.gov

"Sugar Glider USDA." PetSugarGliders.com.
www.petsugargliders.com/sgusda

North American Sugar Glider Association.
www.mynasga.org

Sugar Glider Breeders.
www.sugargliderhelp.com

United Kingdom Websites:

Animal Welfare Act 2006. Legislation.gov.uk.
www.legislation.gov.uk/ukpga/2006/45/contents

"UK Sugar Glider Breeders."
www.sugarglider-breeder.co.uk

4) *Health Insurance for Sugar Gliders*

United States Websites:

Pet Assure.

www.petassure.com/sugar-glider-insurance

VPI Bird and Exotic Pet Insurance.

www.petinsurance.com

"Where Can You Buy Home Insurance that Allows Exotic Pets?" Insurance Providers.

www.insuranceproviders.com/where-can-you-buy-home-insurance-that-allows-exotic-pets

Guardmypet.com Exotic Pet Insurance.

www.guardmypet.com/exotic-pet-insurance

United Kingdom Websites:

Cliverton Exotic Pet and DWAA Insurance.

www.cliverton.co.uk

Fair Investment Company Exotic Pet Insurance.

www.fairinvestment.co.uk/exotic_pet_insurance

"Exotic Pet and Small Mammal Insurance." Healthy-Pets.co.uk.

www.healthy-pets.co.uk

"Companies that Offer Insurance for Exotic Pets." Which Pet Insurance.

www.whichpetinsurance.co.uk

Exotic Direct Pet Insurance.

www.exoticdirect.co.uk

Appendix B: Recipes for Sugar Glider Food

As an alternative to purchasing commercial sugar glider pellets for your pet, you may want to consider a homemade staple diet. In making your own sugar glider food you have complete control over the ingredients that it contains and you can also customize the diet to suit your sugar glider's individual needs. For example, if your sugar glider is suffering from malnutrition, you can fortify your homemade sugar glider diet recipe with extra vitamins and minerals. This section contains recipes for food that you can make and try on your own sugar gliders.

1) Basic Leadbeaters Diet

This formula was originally developed at the Taronga Zoo in Australia for the feeding of captive possums and other marsupials. The official name for this diet is Leadbeater's Nectar Mix, though it is typically referred to as Leadbeater's Diet or the basic Leadbeater's mixture.

Ingredients:
- 450 ml warm water
- 450 ml honey
- 3 boiled eggs, shell removed
- 75 g high-protein baby cereal
- 3 teaspoons Sustagen vitamin supplement

Directions:
Place the water in a clean container and slowly mix in the honey. In a mixing bowl blend the eggs until they are mushy, add ½ of the water/honey mixture until smooth. Add the remaining water/honey mixture and stir in the baby cereal and Sustagen. Blend for at least 1 minute until smooth and free of lumps.

2) Bourbon's Modified Leadbeater's (BML) Diet

This diet is a modified form of the original Leadbeater's Diet and is one of the most popular diets for sugar gliders currently in use. When preparing this diet, be sure to follow the ingredients and instructions carefully because if you make any changes, your sugar glider may not eat it.

Ingredients:
- ½ cup dry baby cereal
- ½ cup honey
- ¼ cup unsweetened apple juice
- ¼ cup wheat germ
- 4 oz. premixed Gerber Mixed Fruit with Yogurt juice
- 2 (2 ½ oz.) jars chicken baby food
- 2 teaspoons non-phosphorus calcium supplement with Vitamin D_3
- 1 teaspoon vitamin supplement
- 1 boiled egg, shell removed

Directions:
Combine the honey, egg and juice in a blender until smooth. Add the remaining ingredients and blend for 4 to 5 minutes until well combined. Pour the mixture into ice cube trays and freeze. Thaw and use as required.

3) Exotic Diet Plan

This diet plan is easier to prepare than Leadbeater's mixture but requires additional supplementation. If you plan to use this recipe, you should add additional protein such as chicken or eggs several nights per week and supplement with fresh fruits and vegetables.

Ingredients:
- 25 oz. unsweetened apple sauce
- 4 oz. non-fat plain yogurt
- 3 oz. concentrated orange juice (calcium fortified)
- ¾ cup old-fashioned oats
- 1 tablespoon ground wheat germ

Directions:
Combine all ingredients in a mixing bowl and whisk until well blended. Divide the mixture between 3 bowls and leave one bowl plain. To the second bowl add 3 small scrambled eggs and to the third add ¾ lbs. unsalted boiled chicken (shredded). For the first two feedings, offer the plain mixture fresh, then freeze the remainder in quart-size freezer bags stored flat. Break off pieces of the frozen mixture and serve thawed along with fresh fruits and vegetables.

4) Pockets Modified Leadbeater's (PML) Mix

This recipe is a good basic diet that can be supplemented with live insects, fruits and vegetables. Follow the directions carefully during preparation to avoid compromising the nutritional content of the ingredients.

Ingredients:

- 1 ¾ cups bottled water
- 1 ¾ cups honey
- 2 boiled eggs, shell removed
- 1 ounce Wombaroo high-protein supplement

Directions:

Heat the water in the microwave for 2 minutes until warm. Do not boil, as this will destroy the vitamins in the Wombaroo supplement when added. Whisk in the honey until dissolved, transfer to a blender along with the eggs and lend for 1 minute. Add the Wombaroo supplement and blend for another minute until smooth. Freeze the mixture in small ice cube trays – 1 tablespoon is the ideal portion size per glider. Offer this mixture thawed along with 1 tablespoon insectivore mix and 1 tablespoon each fresh fruits and vegetables.

Index

D

E

F

G

H

I

J

T

U

V

W

Y

Notes

CPSIA information can be obtained at www.ICGtesting.com
Printed in the USA
LVOW01s1538050215

425838LV00001B/174/P